A Visit from the Aliens

Contents

A Visit from the Aliens

Brandon Robshaw

Published in association with
The Basic Skills Agency

Hodder & S...

A MEMBER OF THE HODD...

Acknowledgements
Cover: Fred Van Deelen
Illustrations: Jo Blake/Beehive Illustrations

Orders; please contact Bookpoint Ltd, 39 Milton Park, Abingdon, Oxon OX14
4TD. Telephone: (44) 01235 400414, Fax: (44) 01235 400454. Lines are open
from 9.00–6.00, Monday to Saturday, with a 24 hour message answering service.
Email address: orders@bookpoint.co.uk

British Library Cataloguing in Publication Data
A catalogue record for this title is available from the British Library

ISBN 0 340 77677 3

First published 2000
Impression number 10 9 8 7 6 5 4 3 2 1
Year   2005 2004 2003 2002 2001 2000

Copyright © 2000 Brandon Robshaw

Typeset by GreenGate Publishing Services, Tonbridge, Kent.
Printed in Great Britain for Hodder and Stoughton Educational, a division of
Hodder Headline Plc, 338 Euston Road, London NW1 3BH, by Atheneum
Press, Gateshead, Tyne & Wear

1

The Island

Steve would never forget
the day the aliens landed.
He was there.
Most people only saw it on television.
Steve was right there.
This is how it happened.

The aliens told us they were coming.
They sent radio messages from deep space.

'We're coming to visit you,' they said.
A friendly visit. We come in peace.
Would next Friday be all right?'

Everyone on Earth got very excited.
There was a lot of talk
about where the aliens should land.
The Americans said it should be the USA.
The Russians said it should be Russia.
The Chinese said it should be China
and so on.

In the end, somebody had a good idea.
An island was built for the aliens.
A square kilometre of steel and plastic.
Right in the middle of the sea.
'Land here,' we told them.

The leaders of all the nations were there.
Prime Ministers, Presidents,
Kings and Queens.
The leader of the United Nations was there.

The head of NASA was there.
Scientists of all nations were there.
So were soldiers.
Just in case the aliens turned nasty.

Then there were all the useful people.
Cooks, cleaners, nurses and odd-jobbers.
That was how Steve got to be there.
He was a cook.
Well, he was learning to be a cook.
He was seventeen years old.
He was still at catering college.
It was just a stroke of luck
that he'd been picked to go on the island.
It was his job to help feed all the VIPs
and the aliens, when they arrived.

So that was how Steve came to be
on an island of steel and plastic
in the middle of the sea.
Looking up at the sky,
waiting for the aliens.

2

The Landing

In the middle of the island
was a landing pad.
Around it,
the leaders of all the nations stood waiting.
Flags flew in the breeze.

Steve was at the back
with the other workers.
Everyone was looking up at the sky.

Suddenly, Steve saw it.
He pointed.
'Look! They're coming!'

High up in the sky was a tiny silver dot.
It was getting bigger by the second.
Everyone was pointing now.
Now the dot was a silver circle.
Then it was a giant silver ball.
It came down so fast,
Steve thought it would smash
the island to pieces.

At the last second, it slowed right down.
It came to rest gently on the landing pad.
A great big silver ball,
the size of an ocean liner.

Steve felt excited.
His heart was beating fast.
What would the aliens be like?

Slowly, the door of the spaceship opened.

3

The Aliens

The aliens came out.
They were very big –
as big as elephants.
They walked on two legs
and had broad, flat
bright pink faces.
They wore loose clothes,
like pyjamas, in bright colours –
red and orange and yellow and green and blue.

There were ten of them.
They came out of the spaceship
and stood there, looking around.
Then the biggest one spoke.
It had a loud voice.
'Hello everyone,' it said.
'We come in peace.'

Steve wondered where
it had learned English.
Maybe the aliens had picked up
radio and television from Earth
out in space.
Yes, that must be it.

The President of the USA
came forward.
He stood on a platform.
He began his welcome speech.

'Welcome to Earth, friends.
For we are your friends.
For years, we have dreamed of this day –
to greet visitors from another world.
You have travelled millions of miles
to be with us today ...'

Steve had already heard the speech
at the run-through the day before.
He thought it was very boring.

It turned out that the aliens agreed.
One of them, dressed in red,
stepped forward.
'Please be quiet,' it said.
'You must stop talking.'

The President stopped.
His mouth stayed open.
He looked puzzled.
No one had ever told him
to stop talking before.

'On our planet,' said the alien,
'it is rude to make speeches.'

'We come in peace,' said another alien.
'But there will be no peace
if you are rude to us.'

'I – I'm sorry,' said the President.
He got down from the platform.
He looked very hurt.
He had spent days writing that speech.

The leaders of all the nations
looked at each other.
They had wanted to make speeches too.
What were they going to do now?

4

Gifts

The leader of the United Nations took over.
He stepped up and spoke to the aliens.
'We'll skip the speeches, then,' he said.
Steve wasn't sorry about that.

'We're sorry we offended you,'
said the leader of the UN.
'Let's go on to the gifts.'

All the countries of the world
had brought gifts for the aliens.
There were carpets from Turkey,
wines from France,
jewels from India,
a car from America.
The British were giving
a picture of the Queen.

'What?' said an alien dressed in green.
'What do you mean, gifts?'
It sounded very angry, thought Steve.

'Well – presents,' said the leader of the UN.
'Things we want to give you.'

The aliens waved their arms around
and stamped their feet.
They looked terribly angry.
It was a frightening sight.

'On our planet
we only give gifts to beggars!'
said the alien in green.

'Are you calling us beggars?'
said another alien, dressed in orange.
'That's an insult!'

'You'd better be polite,'
said the biggest alien,
'or there'll be trouble!'

5

The Banquet

'No, please – we don't want trouble!'
said the leader of the UN.
'We'll forget the gifts. We're very sorry.'

The aliens stopped stamping and waving.
'All right,' said the biggest alien.
'But you'd better not
insult us again.'
The leader of the UN didn't know what to say.
He stepped down off the platform.

Nobody else knew what to say either.
Then the head of NASA came forward.
He spoke to the aliens.
'Let's move on to the banquet,' he said.
'Sit down and eat with us.
We've got all kinds of food.'

This was true.
Steve had helped to cook the banquet.
There was steak in case the aliens ate meat.
There was tuna in case they ate fish.
There were carrots in case
they were vegetarians.
There were noodles in case they ate noodles.
There was chocolate in case they ate
sweet things, and ice cream
in case they ate cold things.
There was food from all over the world.
There had to be something they would like,
thought Steve.

But the aliens didn't look pleased.
They were starting to wave their hands again.
'Did you say eat with you?'
asked the alien in red.

'Yes,' said the NASA boss.
'On our planet, it's a
way of making people feel at home.'

'On our planet, it's an insult!'
shouted the alien in green.
'We never eat in public.
Only animals do that!'

'You have insulted us three times,'
said the biggest alien.
'This is your last chance.
If you don't welcome us properly –
it will mean war!'

6

A Tense Moment

No one wanted a war with the aliens.
Their science was far ahead of ours.
You only had to look at
their spaceship to see that.
We wouldn't stand a chance in a war.

No one knew what to do.
No one knew what to say.
The President of the USA said nothing.
The leader of the UN said nothing.
The head of NASA said nothing.

'We're waiting,' said the alien in green.
'Welcome us properly –
or it's war!'

The leaders of all the nations
looked at each other.
Everyone was afraid to speak.
No one wanted to say the wrong thing
and get the Earth blown up.
It was a tense moment.

Then Steve had an idea.
He pushed through to the front.
It wasn't his job to speak
but no one else was saying anything.

'We don't know the ways
of your planet,' he said.
'Just tell us how to welcome you
and we'll do it.'

The aliens turned towards Steve.
Their big pink faces stared at him.
'Don't know?' said the alien in blue.
'There is only one way
to welcome visitors.
Your leaders must strip off
and swim in the sea.'

7

A Swim

The leaders looked unhappy.
None of them wanted to strip off in public.
There were TV cameras on the island.
Millions of people would watch them
stripping off.
It was enough to make anyone shy.

None of them wanted to swim in the sea.
It was a cold, windy day.
Much too cold for swimming.
What if there were sharks?

'We're waiting,' said the alien in orange.

'You really want to swim?'
asked the head of NASA.

'No, we don't have to swim,'
said the alien in green.
'We're the visitors.
You have to swim for us.'

'With no clothes on,'
said the alien in red.
'Hurry up,' said the biggest alien.
'Or it's war!'

There was no choice.
Slowly, the Earth leaders
took off their clothes.
Soon, all the Presidents and Prime Ministers,
the Kings and the Queens
were standing there naked.

They didn't look at each other.
They looked down at the ground.

21

They went to the edge of the island.
They jumped into the cold blue water.
They splashed about, gasping with cold.

The aliens watched.
As they watched,
they made a funny snorting noise.
Maybe they're saying something
in their own language, thought Steve.
He wondered what they were saying.

23

8

Goodbye

The leaders splashed about for a few minutes.
'All right,
you can come out now,'
said the alien in yellow.

Shivering with cold,
the leaders climbed out.
Helpers ran and gave them their clothes.
The aliens watched.
They were still making
that funny snorting noise.

'We must go now,'
said the biggest alien.
'Nice to meet you.'

'But – aren't you going to stay?'
asked the President of the USA.
'Now that we've welcomed you?'

'No,' said the biggest alien.
'On our planet,
it's time to go
after the welcome.'

'But – you will come back, won't you?'
asked the head of NASA.

'Maybe,' said the alien in blue.
'If we're not too busy.'

The aliens turned and went back
into their spaceship.
They were snorting loudly.
The door closed behind them.

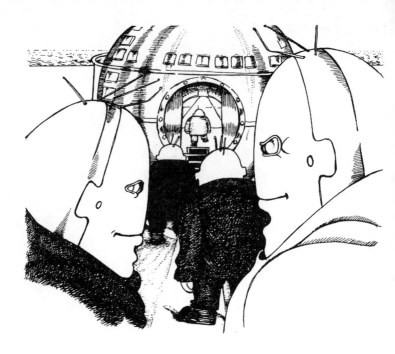

Then the spaceship rose in the air.
Soon it was a little silver circle.
Then it was a little silver dot.
Then it was gone.

Then Steve realised
what the snorting had sounded like.
It had sounded like laughter.

9

Time to go Home

The aliens sat in their space ship, laughing.

'That was a good one,'
said the alien in red.

'Best laugh I've had for ages!'
said the alien in blue.

'Their faces!'
said the alien in orange.
'When they had to strip off
and jump in the sea.'

'Can't we do it again?'
said the alien in green.
'Let's find another planet–
let's have a laugh there, too!'

The biggest alien shook his head.
'Sorry, guys,' he said.
'I've got to get this spaceship
back in the garage
before my dad gets home.
He'll go mad if he find out
we've taken it.
You know what parents are like.'

The other aliens nodded sadly.
They knew what parents were like.